PENGUIN BOOKS

Poems and Readings for Weddings

Julia Watson was born in Wales, and read English and Drama at Exeter University.

Her many television appearances include several series of *Casualty* for the BBC playing Dr Baz – she recently paid a final visit to Holby! – and Thames TV's long-running comedy series *Never the Twain* with Donald Sinden and Windsor Davies. She has worked extensively in theatre, and has appeared in *Danton's Death, Major Barbara, She Stoops to Conquer* and *Wild Honey* for the National Theatre.

In 2003 she received a Grammy nomination (Best Performance) for *The Woman and the Hare* with the Nashe Ensemble.

Julia Watson is married to the poet David Harsent. They live with their daughter in Barnes, south-west London.

Poems and Readings for Weddings

EDITED BY JULIA WATSON

PENGUIN BOOKS

PENGUIN BOOKS

UK | USA | Canada | Ireland | Australia
India | New Zealand | South Africa

Penguin Books is part of the Penguin Random House group of companies
whose addresses can be found at global.penguinrandomhouse.com.

 Penguin
Random House
UK

First published in Penguin Books 2004
Published in this edition 2020

025

Printed and bound in Great Britain by Clays Ltd, Elcograf S.p.A.

A CIP catalogue record for this book is available from the British Library

ISBN: 978-0-141-01495-1

Contents

O tell me the truth about love . . .

'And what of Marriage, master?'

Foreword

I got married in the local Register Office: a drab room in a drab part of London with the service – if you could call it that – conducted in a rather perfunctory manner. After it was all over, in what felt like a matter of seconds, I remember thinking, 'Is that it? Is that what represents the major commitment I have made to someone today?'

The wedding had been organized in something of a rush, and, no, it wasn't because I was pregnant, but because my work schedule kept getting in the way of longer-term planning. With much to do in a short space of time, we didn't think to extend the ritual and give it more weight by having readings. I have always regretted not planning the service more carefully and making it more personal. At the time I was struck by how passive the roles of bride and bridegroom are within the ceremony; by adding readings, and perhaps music, we would have been able to claim it as more our own.

From time to time I have been asked to read at friends' weddings or to suggest an appropriate reading. Inevitably, the same poems and texts come to mind; and it was in searching for something less common that the idea for this collection came about. I have tried to include as many different 'voices' as possible; there are no rules as to who should read or how many readings there should be. The bride or groom might decide they want to say something apart from 'I do'. Their choice would, of course, be different from a reading given by an old friend of the family or a bridesmaid. Nowadays people get married at different stages of their lives and perhaps more than once, so this collection is as broad as possible. Some of the very short pieces are also suggestions for inclusion on a printed order of service.

If you are the person giving the reading, my advice, as a professional actress, is to make sure you know it very well. If it's a poem, that means checking the rhythm of the verse as well as being very clear about its sense. Pick something you are comfortable with. I was once at a wedding where a young girl, with a very simple but beautiful singing voice, had been asked to sing the bride's favourite aria. Her voice was completely unsuited to the scale and range of the piece and the result was . . . well . . . less than successful.

And – crucially – don't forget to speak up. It might seem obvious but I have attended many weddings where I've strained to hear the reading. If it's to be a church ceremony, there might well be a practice before the event – if possible, go to that and test out the acoustics of the space. Otherwise, as a rough rule of thumb, speak to the people at the back. If they can hear you, everyone can. After all, the reading has been chosen by the bride and groom to say something about how they view their commitment to each other. It needs to be heard.

Julia Watson

Love is enough . . .

May your hands be for ever clasped in friendship
And your hearts joined for ever in love

                                        Anon.

Love is Enough

Love is enough: though the World be a-waning,
And the woods have no voice but the voice of complaining,
   Though the sky be too dark for dim eyes to discover
The gold-cups and daisies fair blooming thereunder,
Though the hills be held shadows, and the sea a dark wonder,
   And this day draw a veil over all deeds pass'd over,
Yet their hands shall not tremble, their feet shall not falter;
The void shall not weary, the fear shall not alter
   These lips and these eyes of the loved and the lover.

William Morris (1834–96)

'That is the true season of love'

That is the true season of love, when we believe that we alone can love, that no one could ever have loved so before us, and that no one will ever love in the same way after us.

Johann Wolfgang von Goethe (1749–1832),
translated from the German by Otto Wenckstern

A Spring Morning

The spring comes in with all her hues and smells,
In freshness breathing over hills and dells;
O'er woods where May her gorgeous drapery flings,
And meads washed fragrant by their laughing springs.
Fresh as new opened flowers untouched and free
From the bold rifling of the amorous bee.
The happy time of singing birds is come,
And love's lone pilgrimage now finds a home;
Amongst the mossy oaks now coos the dove,
And the hoarse crow finds softer notes for love.
The foxes play around their dens, and bark
In joy's excess, 'mid woodland shadows dark;
The flowers join lips below; the leaves above;
And every sound that meets the ear is love.

John Clare (1793–1864)

'Let me not to the marriage of true minds'

Let me not to the marriage of true minds
Admit impediments; love is not love
Which alters when it alteration finds,
Or bends with the remover to remove.
O, no, it is an ever-fixed mark,
That looks on tempests and is never shaken;
It is the star to every wand'ring bark,
Whose worth's unknown, although his height be taken.
Love's not Time's fool, though rosy lips and cheeks
Within his bending sickle's compass come;
Love alters not with his brief hours and weeks,
But bears it out even to the edge of doom.
   If this be error and upon me proved,
    I never writ, nor no man ever loved.

William Shakespeare (1564–1616)

The Master Speed

No speed of wind or water rushing by
But you have speed far greater. You can climb
Back up a stream of radiance to the sky,
And back through history up the stream of time.
And you were given this swiftness, not for haste
Nor chiefly that you may go where you will,
But in the rush of everything to waste,
That you may have the power of standing still –
Off any still or moving thing you say.
Two such as you with such a master speed
Cannot be parted nor be swept away
From one another once you are agreed
That life is only life forevermore
Together wing to wing and oar to oar.

Robert Frost (1874–1963)

'If love is chaste'

If love is chaste, if pity comes from heaven,
If fortune, good or ill, is shared between
Two equal loves, and if one wish can govern
Two hearts, and nothing evil intervene;
If one soul joins two bodies fast for ever,
And if, on the same wings, those two can fly,
And if one dart of love can pierce and sever
The vital organs of both equally;
If both love one another with the same
Passion, and if each other's good is sought
By both, if taste and pleasure and desire
Bind such a faithful love-knot, who can claim,
Either with envy, scorn, contempt or ire,
The power to untie so fast a knot?

Michelangelo (1475–1564),
translated from the Italian by
Elizabeth Jennings

'No love, to love of man and wife'

No love, to love of man and wife;
No hope, to hope of constant heart;
No joy, to joy in wedded life;
No faith, to faith in either part:
    Flesh is of flesh, and bone of bone
    When deeds and thoughts and words are one.

Thy friend an other friend may be,
But other self is not the same:
Thy spouse the self-same is with thee,
In body, mind, in goods and name:
    No thine, no mine, may other call,
    Now all is one, and one is all.

Richard Eedes (1555–1604)

A Marriage

A marriage . . . makes of two fractional lives a whole; it gives to two purposeless lives a work, and doubles the strength of each to perform it; it gives to two questioning natures a reason for living, and something to live for; it will give a new gladness to the sunshine, a new fragrance to the flowers, a new beauty to the earth, and a new mystery to life.

Mark Twain (1835–1910)

'And man and woman are like the earth, that brings forth flowers'

And man and woman are like the earth, that brings forth flowers
in summer, and love, but underneath is rock.
Older than flowers, older than ferns, older than foraminiferae,
older than plasm altogether is the soul of a man underneath.

And when, throughout all the wild orgasms of love
slowly a gem forms, in the ancient, once-more-molten rocks
of two human hearts, two ancient rocks, a man's heart and a
      woman's,
that is the crystal of peace, the slow hard jewel of trust,
the sapphire of fidelity.
The gem of mutual peace emerging from the wild chaos of love.

from *'Fidelity'*, D. H. Lawrence (1885–1930)

Changes

Would you marry?
Then you must give everything you have.

Would you marry?
Then everything you have will be what you gain.

Would you marry?
Then you must walk unafraid in a strange land.

Would you marry?
Then be sure that you'll recognize all you see.

Would you marry?
Then you will become as an open book.

Would you marry?
Then you will become a tale yet to be told.

Would you marry?
Then you must sing a different song.

Would you marry?
Then two voices will sing as one.

Mary-Ann Tracey (1934–)

'Live you by love confined'

Live you by love confined,
There is no nearer nearness;
Break not his light bounds,
The stars' and seas' harness:
There is nothing beyond,
We have found the land's end.
We'll take no mortal wound
Who felt him in the furnace,
Drowned in his fierceness,
By his midsummer browned:
Nor ever lose awareness
Of nearness and farness
Who've stood at earth's heart careless
Of suns and storms around,
Who have leant on the hedge of the wind,
On the last ledge of darkness.

We are where love has come
To live: he is that river
Which flows and is the same;
He is not the famous deceiver
Nor early-flowering dream.
Content you. Be at home
In me. There's but one room
Of all the house you may never
Share, deny or enter.
There, as a candle's beam
Stands firm and will not waver
Spire-straight in a close chamber,
As though in shadowy cave a
Stalagmite of flame,
The integral spirit climbs
The dark in light for ever.

from *The Magnetic Mountain*,
C. Day Lewis (1904–72)

Wedding Day

This day of days
Your separate ways
Become one.

This ring, this vow,
Tell you that now
A new life's begun.

Two roads converging
Then, finally, merging
Under the sun.

Good luck holding
A future unfolding
That can't be undone.

Adrian Lomas (1950–)

Friendship

Such love I cannot analyse;
It does not rest in lips or eyes,
Neither in kisses nor caress.
Partly, I know, it's gentleness

And understanding in one word
Or in brief letters. It's preserved
By trust and by respect and awe.
These are the words I'm feeling for.

Two people, yes, two lasting friends.
The giving comes, the taking ends.
There is no measure for such things.
For this all Nature slows and sings.

Elizabeth Jennings (1926–2001)

'love is more thicker than forget'

love is more thicker than forget
more thinner than recall
more seldom than a wave is wet
more frequent than to fail

it is most mad and moonly
and less it shall unbe
than all the sea which only
is deeper than the sea

love is less always than to win
less never than alive
less bigger than the least begin
less littler than forgive

it is most sane and sunly
and more it cannot die
than all the sky which only
is higher than the sky

e. e. cummings (1894–1962)

How do I love thee? . . .

My bounty is as boundless as the sea,
My love as deep; the more I give to thee,
The more I have, for both are infinite.

from *Romeo and Juliet* (II.ii),
William Shakespeare (1564–1616)

'How do I love thee? Let me count the ways'

How do I love thee? Let me count the ways.
I love thee to the depth and breadth and height
My soul can reach, when feeling out of sight
For the ends of Being and ideal Grace.
I love thee to the level of every day's
Most quiet need, by sun and candle-light.
I love thee freely, as men strive for Right;
I love thee purely, as they turn from Praise.
I love thee with the passion put to use
In my old griefs, and with my childhood's faith:
I love thee with a love I seemed to lose
With my lost saints, – I love thee with the breath,
Smiles, tears, of all my life! – and, if God choose,
I shall but love thee better after death.

from *Sonnets from the Portuguese*,
Elizabeth Barrett Browning (1806–61)

Amo Ergo Sum

Because I love
>The sun pours out its rays of living gold
>Pours out its gold and silver on the sea.

Because I love
>The earth upon her astral spindle winds
>Her ecstasy-producing dance.

Because I love
>Clouds travel on the winds through the wide skies,
>Skies wide and beautiful, blue and deep.

Because I love
>Wind blows white sails,
>The wind blows over flowers, the sweet wind blows.

Because I love
>The ferns grow green, and green the grass, and green
>The transparent sunlit trees.

Because I love
>Larks rise up from the grass
>And all the leaves are full of singing birds.

Because I love
>The summer air quivers with a thousand wings,
>Myriads of jewelled eyes burn in the light.

Because I love
>The iridescent shells upon the sand
>Take forms as fine and intricate as thought.

Because I love
     There is an invisible way across the sky,
     Birds travel by that way, the sun and moon
     And all the stars travel that path by night.

Because I love
     There is a river flowing all night long.

Because I love
     All night the river flows into my sleep,
     Ten thousand living things are sleeping in my arms,
     And sleeping wake, and flowing are at rest.

                                    Kathleen Raine (1908–2003)

'Never above you'

Never above you. Never below you. Always beside you.

Walter Winchell (1897–1972)

A Dedication to My Wife

To whom I owe the leaping delight
That quickens my senses in our wakingtime
And the rhythm that governs the repose of our sleepingtime,
    The breathing in unison

Of lovers whose bodies smell of each other
Who think the same thoughts without need of speech
And babble the same speech without need of meaning.

No peevish winter wind shall chill
No sullen tropic sun shall wither
The roses in the rose-garden which is ours and ours only

But this dedication is for others to read:
These are private words addressed to you in public.

T. S. Eliot (1885–1965)

To My Dear and Loving Husband

If ever two were one, then surely we.
If ever man were loved by wife, then thee;
If ever wife was happy in a man,
Compare with me ye women if you can.
I prize thy love more than whole mines of gold,
Or all the riches that the East doth hold.
My love is such that rivers cannot quench,
Nor ought but love from thee, give recompense.
Thy love is such I can no way repay,
The heavens reward thee manifold, I pray.
Then while we live, in love let's so persevere
That when we live no more, we may live ever.

Anne Bradstreet (1612–72)

'Only our love hath no decay'

Only our love hath no decay;
This, no tomorrow hath, nor yesterday,
Running it never runs from us away,
But truly keeps his first, last, everlasting day.

from *'The Anniversary'*,
John Donne (1572–1631)

I Love Thee

I love thee – I love thee!
    'Tis all that I can say;
It is my vision in the night,
    My dreaming in the day;
The very echo of my heart,
    The blessing when I pray:
I love thee – I love thee,
    Is all that I can say.

I love thee – I love thee!
    Is ever on my tongue;
In all my proudest poesy
    That chorus still is sung;
It is the verdict of my eyes,
    Amidst the gay and young:
I love thee – I love thee,
    A thousand maids among.

I love thee – I love thee!
    Thy bright and hazel glance,
The mellow lute upon those lips,
    Whose tender tones entrance;
But most, dear heart of hearts, thy proofs
    That still these words enhance,
I love thee – I love thee;
    Whatever be thy chance.

Thomas Hood (1799–1845)

The Confirmation

Yes, yours, my love, is the right human face.
I in my mind had waited for this long,
Seeing the false and searching for the true,
Then found you as a traveller finds a place
Of welcome suddenly amid the wrong
Valleys and rocks and twisting roads. But you,
What shall I call you? A fountain in a waste,
A well of water in a country dry,
Or anything that's honest and good, an eye
That makes the whole world bright. Your open heart,
Simple with giving, gives the primal deed,
The first good world, the blossom, the blowing seed,
The hearth, the steadfast land, the wandering sea.
Not beautiful or rare in every part.
But like yourself, as they were meant to be.

Edwin Muir (1887–1959)

'Is it for now or for always'

Is it for now or for always,
The world hangs on a stalk?
Is it a trick or a trysting-place,
The woods we have found to walk?

Is it a mirage or miracle,
Your lips that lift at mine:
And the suns like a juggler's juggling-balls,
Are they a sham or a sign?

Shine out, my sudden angel,
Break fear with breast and brow,
I take you now and for always,
For always is always now.

Philip Larkin (1922–85)

Hinterhof

Stay near to me and I'll stay near to you –
As near as you are dear to me will do,
    Near as the rainbow to the rain,
    The west wind to the windowpane,
As fire to the hearth, as dawn to dew.

Stay true to me and I'll stay true to you –
As true as you are new to me will do,
    New as the rainbow in the spray,
    Utterly new in every way,
New in the way that what you say is true.

Stay near to me, stay true to me. I'll stay
As near, as true to you as heart could pray.
    Heart never hoped that one might be
    Half of the things you are to me –
The dawn, the fire, the rainbow and the day.

James Fenton (1949–)

Love Not Me

Love not me for comely grace,
For my pleasing eye or face;
Nor for any outward part,
No, nor for my constant heart:
    For those may fail or turn to ill,
    So thou and I shall sever.
Keep therefore a true woman's eye,
And love me still, but know not why;
    So hast thou the same reason still
    To doat upon me ever.

John Wilbye (1574–1638)

'i carry your heart with me'

i carry your heart with me (i carry it in
my heart) i am never without it (anywhere
i go you go, my dear; and whatever is done
by only me is your doing, my darling)
                                    i fear
no fate (for you are my fate, my sweet) i want
no world (for beautiful you are my world, my true)
and it's you are whatever a moon has always meant
and whatever a sun will always sing is you

here is the deepest secret nobody knows
(here is the root of the root and the bud of the bud
and the sky of the sky of a tree called life; which grows
higher than soul can hope or mind can hide)
and this is the wonder that's keeping the stars apart

i carry your heart (i carry it in my heart)

e.e. cummings (1894–1962)

Love Song

There is a strong wall about me to protect me:
It is built of the words you have said to me.

There are swords about me to keep me safe:
They are the kisses of your lips.

Before me goes a shield to guard me from harm:
It is the shadow of your arms between me and danger.

All the wishes of my mind know your name,
And the white desires of my heart
They are acquainted with you.
The cry of my body for completeness,
That is a cry to you.
My blood beats out your name to me, unceasing, pitiless
Your name, your name.

Mary Carolyn Davies
(late nineteenth/early twentieth century)

'I do not love you as if you were salt-rose, or topaz'

I do not love you as if you were salt-rose, or topaz,
or the arrow of carnations the fire shoots off.
I love you as certain dark things are to be loved,
in secret, between the shadow and the soul.

I love you as the plant that never blooms
but carries in itself the light of hidden flowers;
thanks to your love a certain solid fragrance,
risen from the earth, lives darkly in my body.

I love you without knowing how, or when, or from where.
I love you straightforwardly, without complexities or pride;
so I love you because I know no other way

than this: where *I* does not exist, nor *you*,
so close that your hand on my chest is my hand,
so close that your eyes close as I fall asleep.

Pablo Neruda (1904–73),
translated from the Spanish by Stephen Tapscott

A Birthday

My heart is like a singing bird
   Whose nest is in a watered shoot;
My heart is like an apple-tree
   Whose boughs are bent with thick-set fruit;
My heart is like a rainbow shell
   That paddles in a halcyon sea;
My heart is gladder than all these
   Because my love is come to me.

Raise me a dais of silk and down;
   Hang it with vair and purple dyes;
Carve it in doves, and pomegranates,
   And peacocks with a hundred eyes;
Work it in gold and silver grapes,
   In leaves, and silver fleurs-de-lys;
Because the birthday of my life
   Is come, my love is come to me.

Christina Rossetti (1830–94)

The Bargain

My true love hath my heart, and I have his,
   By just exchange one for another given:
I hold his dear, and mine he cannot miss,
   There never was a better bargain driven:
     My true love hath my heart and I have his.

His heart in me keeps him and me in one,
   My heart in him his thoughts and senses guides:
He loves my heart, for once it was his own,
   I cherish his because in me it bides:
     My true love hath my heart, and I have his.

Sir Philip Sidney (1554–86)

He Wishes for the Cloths of Heaven

Had I the heavens' embroidered cloths,
Enwrought with golden and silver light,
The blue and the dim and the dark cloths
Of night and light and the half-light,
I would spread the cloths under your feet:
But I, being poor, have only my dreams;
I have spread my dreams under your feet;
Tread softly because you tread on my dreams.

W. B. Yeats (1865–1939)

The Good-Morrow

I wonder, by my troth, what thou and I
    Did, till we loved? were we not weaned till then?
But sucked on country pleasures, childishly?
    Or snored we in the seven sleepers' den?
'Twas so; But this, all pleasures fancies be.
If ever any beauty I did see,
Which I desired, and got, 'twas but a dream of thee.

And now good-morrow to our waking souls,
    Which watch not one another out of fear;
For love, all love of other sights controls
    And makes one little room, an everywhere.
Let sea-discoverers to new worlds have gone,
Let maps to others, worlds on worlds have shown,
Let us possess one world, each hath one, and is one.

My face in thine eye, thine in mine appears,
    And true plain hearts do in the faces rest;
Where can we find two better hemispheres,
    Without sharp North, without declining West?
Whatever dies, was not mixed equally;
If our two loves be one, or, thou and I
Love so alike, that none do slacken, none can die.

John Donne (1572–1631)

37

'Shall I compare thee to a summer's day?'

Shall I compare thee to a summer's day?
Thou art more lovely and more temperate:
Rough winds do shake the darling buds of May,
And summer's lease hath all too short a date:
Sometime too hot the eye of heaven shines,
And often is his gold complexion dimmed;
And every fair from fair sometime declines,
By chance, or nature's changing course, untrimmed;
But thy eternal summer shall not fade,
Or lose possession of that fair thou ow'st;
Nor shall death brag thou wander'st in his shade,
When in eternal lines to time thou grow'st:
    So long as men can breathe, or eyes can see,
    So long lives this, and this gives life to thee.

William Shakespeare (1564–1616)

'. . . *winter will seek us, my love*'

... winter
will seek us, my love,
always
it will seek us, because we know it,
because we do not fear it,
because we have
with us
fire
forever,
we have
earth with us
forever,
spring with us
forever,
and when a leaf
falls
from the climbing vines,
you know, my love,
what name is written
on that leaf,
a name that is yours and mine,
our love name, a single
being, the arrow
that pierced winter,
the invincible love,
the fire of the days,

      ***

as if I had never walked
except with you, my heart,

as if I could not walk
except with you,
as if I could not sing
except when you sing.

from *'Epithalamium'*,
Pablo Neruda (1904–73),
translated from the Spanish by
Donald D. Walsh

Wedding

From time to time our love is like a sail
and when the sail begins to alternate
from tack to tack, it's like a swallowtail
and when the swallow flies it's like a coat;
and if the coat is yours, it has a tear
like a wide mouth and when the mouth begins
to draw the wind, it's like a trumpeter
and when the trumpet blows, it blows like millions . . .
and this, my love, when millions come and go
beyond the need of us, is like a trick;
and when the trick begins, it's like a toe
tip-toeing on a rope, which is like luck;
and when the luck begins, it's like a wedding,
which is like love, which is like everything.

Alice Oswald (1966–)

I Love You

I love you,
Not only for what you are,
But for what I am
When I am with you.

I love you,
Not only for what
You have made of yourself,
But for what
You are making of me.

I love you
For the part of me
That you bring out;
I love you
For putting your hand
Into my heaped-up heart
And passing over
All the foolish, weak things
That you can't help
Dimly seeing there,
And for drawing out
Into the light
All the beautiful belongings
That no one else had looked
Quite far enough to find.

I love you because you
Are helping me to make
Of the lumber of my life
Not a tavern
But a temple;

Out of the works
Of my every day
Not a reproach
But a song.

I love you
Because you have done
More than any creed
Could have done
To make me good,
And more than any fate
Could have done
To make me happy.

You have done it
Without a touch
Without a word,
Without a sign.
You have done it
By being yourself.
Perhaps that is what
Being a friend means,
After all.

Roy Croft (1907–73)

'You and I'

You and I
Have so much love
That it
Burns like a fire,
In which we bake a lump of clay
Molded into a figure of you
And a figure of me.
Then we take both of them,
And break them into pieces,
And mix the pieces with water,
And mold again a figure of you,
And a figure of me.
I am in your clay.
In life we share a single quilt.
In death we will share one bed.

Kuan Tao-Sheng (1262–1319),
translated from the Chinese by
Kenneth Rexroth and
Ling Chung

I Would Live in Your Love

I would live in your love as the sea-grasses live in the sea,
Borne up by each wave as it passes, drawn down by each wave
    that recedes;
I would empty my soul of the dreams that have gathered in me,
I would beat with your heart as it beats, I would follow your
    soul as it leads.

Sara Teasdale (1884–1933)

'Everything that touches us, me and you'

Everything that touches us, me and you,
takes us together like a violin's bow,
which draws *one* voice out of two separate strings.
Upon what instrument are we two spanned?
And what musician holds us in his hand?
Oh sweetest song.

from *'Love Song'*, Rainer Maria Rilke (1875–1926),
translated from the German by Stephen Mitchell

'If thou must love me, let it be for nought'

If thou must love me, let it be for nought
Except for love's sake only. Do not say
'I love her for her smile . . . her look . . . her way
Of speaking gently, . . . for a trick of thought
That falls in well with mine, and certes brought
A sense of pleasant ease on such a day' –
For these things in themselves, Belovèd, may
Be changed, or change for thee, – and love, so wrought,
May be unwrought so. Neither love me for
Thine own dear pity's wiping my cheeks dry,
Since one might well forget to weep, who bore
Thy comfort long, and lose thy love thereby!
But love me for love's sake, that evermore
Thou may'st love on, through love's eternity.

from *Sonnets from the Portuguese*,
Elizabeth Barrett Browning (1806–61)

Lines from a Notebook – February 1807

And in Life's noisiest hour,
There whispers still the ceaseless Love of Thee,
The heart's *Self-solace*, and soliloquy.

You mould my Hopes, you fashion me within;
And to the leading Love-throb in the Heart
Thro' all my being, thro' my pulse's beat.
You lie in all my many Thoughts, like Light
Like the fair Light of Dawn, or summer-Eve
On rippling Stream, or cloud-reflecting Lake.

And looking to the Heaven, that bends above you
How oft! I bless the Lot, that made me love you.

Samuel Taylor Coleridge (1772–1834)

Beauty that is Never Old

When buffeted and beaten by life's storms,
When by the bitter cares of life oppressed,
I want no surer haven than your arms,
I want no sweeter heaven than your breast.

When over my life's way there falls the blight
Of sunless days, and nights of starless skies,
Enough for me, the calm and steadfast light
That softly shines within your loving eyes.

The world, for me, and all the world can hold
Is circled by your arms; for me there lies,
Within the lights and shadows of your eyes,
The only beauty that is never old.

James Weldon Johnson (1871–1938)

'Sensual pleasure passes'

Sensual pleasure passes and vanishes in the twinkling of an eye, but the friendship between us, the mutual confidence, the delights of the heart, the enchantment of the soul, these things do not perish and can never be destroyed.

I shall love you until I die.

Voltaire (1694–1778)

The Dance

I would have each couple turn,
join and unjoin, be lost
in the greater turning
of other couples, woven
in the circle of a dance,
the song of long time flowing

over them, so they may return,
turn again, in to themselves
out of desire greater than their own,
belonging to all, to each,
to the dance, and to the song
that moves them through the night.

What is fidelity? To what
does it hold? The point
of departure, or the turning road
that is departure and absence
and the way home? What we are
and what we were once

are far estranged. For those
who would not change, time
is infidelity. But we are married
until death, and are betrothed
to change. By silence, so,
I learn my song. I earn

my sunny fields by absence, once
and to come. And I love you
as I love the dance that brings you
out of the multitude
in which you come and go.
Love changes, and in change is true.

Wendell Berry (1934–)

'O my luve's like a red, red rose'

O my luve's like a red, red rose,
   That's newly sprung in June;
O my luve's like the melodie
   That's sweetly play'd in tune.

As fair art thou, my bonnie lass,
   So deep in luve am I,
And I will luve thee still, my Dear,
   Till a' the seas gang dry.

Till a' the seas gang dry, my Dear,
   And the rocks melt wi' the sun!
And I will luve thee still my Dear,
   While the sands o' life shall run.

from 'A Red, Red, Rose',
Robert Burns (1759–96)

These I Can Promise

I cannot promise you a life of sunshine;
I cannot promise riches, wealth or gold;
I cannot promise you an easy pathway
That leads away from change or growing old.

But I can promise all my heart's devotion
A smile to chase away your tears of sorrow;
A love that's ever true and ever growing;
A hand to hold in yours through each tomorrow.

Mark Twain (1835–1910)

Reply

I cannot swear with any certainty
That I will always feel as I do now,
Loving you with the same fierce ecstasy,
Needing the same your lips upon my brow.
Nor can I promise stars forever bright,
Or vow green leaves will never turn to gold.
I cannot see beyond this present night
To say what promises the dawn may hold.
And yet, I know my heart must follow you
High up to hilltops, low through vales of tears,
Through golden days and days of somber hue.
And love will only deepen with the years,
Becoming sun and shadow, wind and rain,
Wine that grows mellow, bread that will sustain.

Naomi Long Madgett (1923–)

Love's Insight

Take me, accept me, love me as I am;
Love me with my disordered wayward past;
Love me with all the lusts that hold me fast
In bonds of sensuality and shame.
Love me as flesh and blood, not the ideal
Which vainly you imagine me to be;
Love me, the mixed-up creature that you see;
Love not the man you dream of but the real.
And yet they err who say that love is blind.
Beneath my earthy, sordid self your love
Discerns capacities which rise above
The futile passions of my carnal mind.
Love is creative. Your love brings to birth
God's image in the earthiest of earth.

Robert Winnett (1910–89)

Touch the Air Softly

Now touch the air softly, step gently, one, two ...
I'll love you till roses are robin's-egg blue;
I'll love you till gravel is eaten for bread,
And lemons are orange, and lavender's red.

Now touch the air softly, swing gently the broom.
I'll love you till windows are all of a room;
And the table is laid, and the table is bare,
And the ceiling reposes on bottomless air.

I'll love you till heaven rips the stars from his coat,
And the moon rows away in a glass-bottomed boat;
And Orion steps down like a diver below,
And earth is ablaze, and ocean aglow.

So touch the air softly, and swing the broom high.
We will dust the gray mountains, and sweep the blue sky;
And I'll love you as long as the furrow the plow,
As however is ever, and ever is now.

William Jay Smith (1918–)

Relationships

Understanding must be on both sides,
Confidence with confidence, and every talk
Be like a long and needed walk
When flowers are picked, and almost-asides
Exchanged. Love is always like this
Even when there's no touch or kiss.

There are many kinds of relationships
But this is the best, as Plato said –
Even when it begins in a bed,
The gentle touching of hands and lips –
It is from such kindness friendship is made
Often, a thing not to be repaid

Since there is no price, no counting up
This and that, gift. Humility
Is the essential ability
Before the loved object. Oh, we can sip
Something that tastes almost divine
In such pure sharing – yours and mine.

Elizabeth Jennings (1926–2001)

'I loved you first'

I loved you first: but afterwards your love
   Outsoaring mine, sang such a loftier song
As drowned the friendly cooings of my dove.
   Which owes the other most? my love was long,
   And yours one moment seemed to wax more strong;
I loved and guessed at you, you construed me
And loved me for what might or might not be –
   Nay, weights and measures do us both a wrong.
For verily love knows not 'mine' or 'thine';
   With separate 'I' and 'thou' free love has done,
    For one is both and both are one in love:
Rich love knows naught of 'thine that is not mine';
    Both have the strength and both the length thereof,
   Both of us, of the love which makes us one.

Christina Rossetti (1830–94)

Song

Why should your face so please me
That if one little line should stray
Bewilderment would seize me
And drag me down the tortuous way
Out of the noon into the night?
But so, into this tranquil light
You raise me.

How could our minds so marry
That, separate, blunder to and fro,
Make for a point, miscarry,
And blind as headstrong horses go?
Though now they in their promised land
At pleasure travel hand in hand
Or tarry.

This concord is an answer
To questions far beyond our mind
Whose image is a dancer.
All effort is to ease refined
Here, weight is light; this is the dove
Of love and peace, not heartless love
The lancer.

And yet I still must wonder
That such an armistice can be
And life roll by in thunder
To leave this calm with you and me.
This tranquil voice of silence, yes,
This single song of two, this is
A wonder.

Edwin Muir (1887–1959)

'When in disgrace with fortune and men's eyes'

When in disgrace with fortune and men's eyes,
I all alone beweep my outcast state,
And trouble deaf heaven with my bootless cries,
And look upon myself and curse my fate,
Wishing me like to one more rich in hope,
Featured like him, like him with friends possessed,
Desiring this man's art and that man's scope,
With what I most enjoy contented least;
Yet in these thoughts myself almost despising,
Haply I think on thee, and then my state,
(Like to the lark at break of day arising,
From sullen earth), sings hymns at heaven's gate;
    For thy sweet love remember'd such wealth brings
    That then I scorn to change my state with kings.

William Shakespeare (1564–1616)

'I want to be your friend'

I want to be your friend
for ever and ever.
When the hills are all flat
and the rivers are all dry,
when the trees blossom in winter
and the snow falls in summer,
when heaven and earth mingle –
not till then will I part from you.

The Yüeh-Fu (c. first century AD),
    adapted from the translation
of the Chinese by Arthur Waley

Last Love

Love at the closing of our days
is apprehensive and very tender.
Glow brighter, brighter, farewell rays
of one last love in its evening splendour.

Blue shade takes half the world away:
through western clouds alone some light is slanted.
O tarry, O tarry, declining day,
enchantment, let me stay enchanted.

The blood runs thinner, yet the heart
remains as ever deep and tender.
O last belated love, thou art
a blend of joy and of hopeless surrender.

Fyodor Tyutchev (1803–73),
translated from the Russian by Vladimir Nabokov

'From this day forward'

From this day forward,
You shall not walk alone.
My heart will be your shelter,
And my arms will be your home.

Anon.

O tell me the truth about love . . .

One asked a madman if a wife he had.
'A wife?' quoth he. 'I never was so mad.'

Robert Hayman (1575–?)

O Tell Me the Truth about Love

Some say that love's a little boy,
    And some say it's a bird,
Some say it makes the world go round,
    And some say that's absurd,
And when I asked the man next-door,
    Who looked as if he knew,
His wife got very cross indeed,
    And said it wouldn't do.

Does it look like a pair of pyjamas,
    Or the ham in a temperance hotel?
Does its odour remind one of llamas,
    Or has it a comforting smell?
Is it prickly to touch as a hedge is,
    Or soft as eiderdown fluff?
Is it sharp or quite smooth at the edges?
    O tell me the truth about love.

Our history books refer to it
    In cryptic little notes,
It's quite a common topic on
    The Transatlantic boats;
I've found the subject mentioned in
    Accounts of suicides,
And even seen it scribbled on
    The backs of railway-guides.

Does it howl like a hungry Alsatian,
    Or boom like a military band?
Could one give a first-rate imitation
    On a saw or a Steinway Grand?
Is its singing at parties a riot?

Does it only like Classical stuff?
Will it stop when one wants to be quiet?
O tell me the truth about love.

I looked inside the summer-house;
        It wasn't ever there;
I tried the Thames at Maidenhead,
        And Brighton's bracing air.
I don't know what the blackbird sang,
        Or what the tulip said;
But it wasn't in the chicken-run,
        Or underneath the bed.

Can it pull extraordinary faces?
    Is it usually sick on a swing?
Does it spend all its time at the races,
    Or fiddling with pieces of string?
Has it views of its own about money?
    Does it think Patriotism enough?
Are its stories vulgar but funny?
    O tell me the truth about love.

When it comes, will it come without warning
    Just as I'm picking my nose?
Will it knock on my door in the morning,
    Or tread in the bus on my toes?
Will it come like a change in the weather?
    Will its greeting be courteous or rough?
Will it alter my life altogether?
    O tell me the truth about love.

W. H. Auden (1907–73)

To Wed or Not to Wed

To wed, or not to wed: that is the question:
Whether 'tis nobler in the mind to suffer
The fret and loneliness of spinsterhood
Or to take arms against the single state
And by marrying, end it? To wed; to match,
No more; yet by this match to say we end
The heartache and the thousand natural shocks
That flesh is heir to; 'tis a consummation
Devoutly to be wish'd. To wed, to match;
To match, perchance mismatch: aye there's the rub;
For in that match what dread mishaps may come,
When we have shuffled off this single state
For wedded bliss: there's the respect
That makes singleness of so long a life,
For who'd forgo the joys of wife and mother,
The pleasures of devotion, of sacrifice and love,
The blessings of a home and all home means,
The restful sympathy of soul to soul,
The loving ones circling round at eventide
When she herself might gain all these
With a marriage vow? . . .

(With apologies to Shakespeare)

Una Marson (1905–65)

'I may by degrees dwindle into a wife'

I'll never marry, unless I am first made sure of my will and pleasure . . .

My dear liberty, shall I leave thee? My faithful solitude, my darling contemplation, must I bid you then adieu? Ay-h adieu – my morning thoughts, agreeable wakings, indolent slumbers, all ye *douceurs*, ye *sommeils du matin*, adieu. – I can't do it, 'tis more than impossible. – Positively, Mirabell, I'll lie a-bed in a morning as long as I please . . .

And d'ye hear? I won't be called names after I'm married; positively I won't be call'd names . . . Aye, as wife, spouse, my dear, joy, jewel, love, sweetheart, and the rest of that nauseous cant, in which men and their wives are so fulsomely familiar, – I shall never bear that. – Good Mirabell, don't let us be familiar or fond, nor kiss before folks, like my Lady Fadler and Sir Francis: nor go to Hyde Park together the first Sunday in a new chariot, to provoke eyes and whispers; and then never be seen there together again, as if we were proud of one another the first week, and ashamed of one another ever after. Let us never visit together, nor go to a play together, but let us be very strange and wellbred: let us be as strange as if we had been married a great while; and as wellbred as if we were not married at all . . .

Any more conditions? . . . Trifles, – as liberty to pay and receive visits to and from whom I please; to write and receive letters, without interrogatories or wry faces on your part; to wear what I please; and choose conversation with regard only to my own taste; to have no obligation upon me to converse with wits that I don't like, because they are your acquaintance; or to be intimate with fools, because they may be your relations. Come to dinner when I please, dine in my dressing-room when I'm out of humour, without giving a reason. To have my closet inviolate; to be sole empress of my tea-table, which you must never presume to approach without first asking leave. And lastly, wherever I am, you shall always knock at the door before you come in. These articles subscribed, if I continue to endure you a little longer, I may by degrees dwindle into a wife.

from *The Way of the World* (IV. i), William Congreve (1670–1729)

To the Virgins, to Make Much of Time

Gather ye rosebuds while ye may,
   Old Time is still a-flying:
And this same flower that smiles today
   Tomorrow will be dying.

The glorious lamp of heaven, the sun,
   The higher he's a-getting,
The sooner will his race be run,
   And nearer he's to setting.

That age is best which is the first,
   When youth and blood are warmer;
But being spent, the worse, and worst
   Times still succeed the former.

Then be not coy, but use your time:
   And while ye may go marry;
For having lost but once your prime,
   You may for ever tarry.

Robert Herrick (1591–1674)

The Owl and the Pussy-Cat

The Owl and the Pussy-Cat went to sea
   In a beautiful pea-green boat,
They took some honey, and plenty of money,
   Wrapped up in a five-pound note,
The Owl looked up to the stars above,
   And sang to a small guitar,
'O lovely Pussy, O Pussy, my love,
   What a beautiful Pussy you are,
         You are,
         You are!
   What a beautiful Pussy you are!'

Pussy said to the Owl, 'You elegant fowl!
   How charmingly sweet you sing!
O let us be married! too long we have tarried:
   But what shall we do for a ring?'
They sailed away, for a year and a day,
   To the land where the Bong-tree grows;
And there in a wood a Piggy-wig stood,
   With a ring at the end of his nose,
         His nose,
         His nose,
   With a ring at the end of his nose.

'Dear Pig, are you willing to sell for one shilling
   Your ring?' Said the Piggy, 'I will.'
So they took it away, and were married next day
   By the Turkey who lives on the hill.
They dined on mince and slices of quince,
   Which they ate with a runcible spoon;

And hand in hand, on the edge of the sand,
   They danced by the light of the moon,
        The moon,
        The moon,
   They danced by the light of the moon.

Edward Lear (1812—88)

'O Donald! Ye are just the man'

O Donald! Ye are just the man
   Who, when he's got a wife,
Begins to fratch – nae notice ta-en –
   They're strangers a' their life.

The fan may drop – she takes it up,
   The husband keeps his chair;
She hands the kettle – gives his cup –
   Without e'en – 'Thank ye, dear.'

Now, truly, these slights are but toys;
   But frae neglects like these,
The wife may soon a slattern grow,
   And strive nae mair to please.

For wooers ay do all they can
   To trifle wi' the mind;
They hold the blaze of beauty up,
   And keep the poor things blind.

But wedlock tears away the veil,
   The goddess is nae mair;
He thinks his wife a silly thing,
   She thinks her man a bear.

Let then the lover be the friend –
   The loving friend for life;
Think but thysel the happiest spouse,
   She'll be the happiest wife.

Susanna Blamire (1747–94)

The Author to His Wife, of a Woman's Eloquence

My Mall, I mark that when you mean to prove me
To buy a velvet gown, or some rich border,
Thou call'st me good sweet heart, thou swear'st to love me,
Thy locks, thy lips, thy looks, speak all in order,
Thou think'st and right thou think'st, that these do move me,
That all these severally thy suit do further:
But shall I tell thee what most thy suit advances?
Thy fair smooth words? no, no, thy fair smooth haunches.

Sir John Harington (1561–1612)

I'll Still be Loving You

When your hair has turned to winter
and your teeth are in a plate,
when your getter up and go
has gone to stop and wait –
I'll still be loving you.

When your attributes have shifted
beyond the bounds of grace,
I'll count your many blessings,
not the wrinkles in your face –
I'll still be loving you.

When the crackle in your voice
matches that within your knee
and the times are getting frequent
that you don't remember me –
I'll still be loving you.

Growing old is not a sin,
it's something we all do.
I hope you'll always understand –
I'll still be loving you.

C. David Hay (1936–)

The Passionate Shepherd to His Love

Come live with me and be my Love,
And we will all the pleasures prove
That hills and valleys, dales and fields,
Or woods or steepy mountain yields.

And we will sit upon the rocks
And see the shepherds feed their flocks
By shallow rivers, to whose falls
Melodious birds sing madrigals.

And I will make thee beds of roses
And a thousand fragrant posies,
A cap of flowers and a kirtle
Embroidered all with leaves of myrtle.

A gown made of the finest wool,
Which from our pretty lambs we pull;
Fair-linèd slippers for the cold,
With buckles of the purest gold.

A belt of straw and ivy-buds,
With coral clasps and amber studs:
And if these pleasures may thee move,
Come live with me and be my Love.

The shepherds' swains shall dance and sing
For thy delight each May morning:
If these delights thy mind may move,
Then live with me and be my Love.

Christopher Marlowe (1564–93)

The Nymph's Reply to the Shepherd

If all the world and love were young,
And truth in every shepherd's tongue,
These pretty pleasures might me move
To live with thee and be thy Love.

Time drives the flocks from field to fold,
When rivers rage and rocks grow cold,
And Philomel becometh dumb;
The rest complains of cares to come.

The flowers do fade, and wanton fields
To wayward Winter reckoning yields:
A honey tongue, a heart of gall,
Is fancy's spring, but sorrow's fall.

Thy gowns, thy shoes, thy beds of roses,
Thy cap, thy kirtle, and thy posies
Soon break, soon wither – soon forgotten,
In folly ripe, in reason rotten.

Thy belt of straw and ivy buds,
Thy coral clasps and amber studs, –
All these in me no means can move
To come to thee and be thy Love.

But could youth last and love still breed,
Had joys no date nor age no need,
Then these delights my mind might move
To live with thee and be thy Love.

Sir Walter Ralegh (?1554–1618)

From the Irish

According to Dinneen, a Gael unsurpassed
In lexicographical enterprise, the Irish
For moon means the white circle in a slice
Of half-boiled potato or turnip; a star
Is the mark on the forehead of a beast
And the sun is the bottom of a lake, or well.

Well, if I say to you, your face
Is like a slice of half-boiled turnip,
Your hair is the colour of a lake's bottom.
And at the centre of each of your eyes
Is the mark of the beast, it is because
I want to love you properly, according to Dinneen.

Ian Duhig (1954–)

Love is . . .

Love is feeling cold in the back of vans
Love is a fanclub with only two fans
Love is walking holding paintstained hands
Love is

Love is fish and chips on winter nights
Love is blankets full of strange delights
Love is when you don't put out the light
Love is

Love is the presents in Christmas shops
Love is when you're feeling Top of the Pops
Love is what happens when the music stops
Love is

Love is white panties lying all forlorn
Love is a pink nightdress still slightly warm
Love is when you have to leave at dawn
Love is

Love is you and love is me
Love is a prison and love is free
Love's what's there when you're away from me
Love is . . .

Adrian Henri (1932–2000)

The Female of the Species

When the Himalayan peasant meets the he-bear in his pride,
He shouts to scare the monster, who will often turn aside.
But the she-bear thus accosted rends the peasant tooth and nail
For the female of the species is more deadly than the male.

When Nag the basking cobra hears the careless foot of man,
He will sometimes wriggle sideways and avoid it if he can.
But his mate makes no such motion where she camps beside the
    trail.
For the female of the species is more deadly than the male.

When the early Jesuit fathers preached to Hurons and Choctaws,
They prayed to be delivered from the vengeance of the squaws.
'Twas the women, not the warriors, turned those stark
    enthusiasts pale.
For the female of the species is more deadly than the male.

Man's timid heart is bursting with the things he must not say,
For the Woman that God gave him isn't his to give away;
But when hunter meets with husband, each confirms the other's
    tale –
The female of the species is more deadly than the male.

Man, a bear in most relations – worm and savage otherwise, –
Man propounds negotiations, Man accepts the compromise.
Very rarely will he squarely push the logic of a fact
To its ultimate conclusion in unmitigated act.

Fear, or foolishness, impels him, ere he lay the wicked low,
To concede some form of trial even to his fiercest foe.
Mirth obscene diverts his anger – Doubt and Pity oft perplex
Him in dealing with an issue – to the scandal of The Sex!

But the Woman that God gave him, every fibre of her frame
Proves her launched for one sole issue, armed and engined for
    the same;
And to serve that single issue, lest the generations fail,
The female of the species must be deadlier than the male.

She who faces Death by torture for each life beneath her breast
May not deal in doubt or pity – must not swerve for fact or jest.
These be purely male diversions – not in these her honour
    dwells.
She, the Other Law we live by, is that Law and nothing else.

She can bring no more to living than the powers that make her
    great
As the Mother of the Infant and the Mistress of the Mate.
And when Babe and Man are lacking and she strides unclaimed
    to claim
Her right as femme (and baron), her equipment is the same.

She is wedded to convictions – in default of grosser ties;
Her contentions are her children, Heaven help him who
    denies! –
He will meet no suave discussion, but the instant, white-hot,
    wild,
Wakened female of the species warring as for spouse and child.

Unprovoked and awful charges – even so the she-bear fights,
Speech that drips, corrodes, and poisons – even so the cobra
    bites,
Scientific vivisection of one nerve till it is raw
And the victim writhes in anguish – like the Jesuit with the
    squaw!

So it comes that Man, the coward, when he gathers to confer
With his fellow-braves in council, dare not leave a place for her
Where, at war with Life and Conscience, he uplifts his erring
    hands
To some God of Abstract Justice – which no woman
    understands.

And Man knows it! Knows, moreover, that the Woman that
    God gave him
Must command but may not govern – shall enthral but not
    enslave him.
And *She* knows, because She warns him, and Her instincts never
    fail,
That the Female of Her Species is more deadly than the Male.

Rudyard Kipling (1865–1936)

Always Marry an April Girl

Praise the spells and bless the charms,
I found April in my arms
April golden, April cloudy,
Gracious, cruel, tender, rowdy;
April soft in flowered langour,
April cold in sudden anger,
Ever changing, ever true —
I love April, I love you.

Ogden Nash (1902–71)

I'll be There

I'll be there, my darling,
Through thick and through thin
When your mind is a mess
When your head's in a spin
When your plane's been delayed
When you've missed the last train
When life is just threatening
To drive you insane
When your thrilling whodunnit
Has lost its last page
When somebody tells you
You're looking your age
When your coffee's too cool
And your wine is too warm
When the forecast said 'Fine'
But you're out in a storm
When you ordered the korma
But got the Madras
When you wake in the night
And are sure you smell gas
When your quick-break hotel
Is more like a slum
And your holiday photos
Show only your thumb
When you park for five minutes
In a residents' bay
And return to discover
You've been towed away
When the jeans that you bought
In hope or in haste

Stick on your hips
And won't reach round your waist
When the dentist looks into
Your mouth and just sighs
When your heroes turn out
To be wimps in disguise
When the food you most like
Brings you out in red rashes
When as soon as you boot up
The bloody thing crashes
When you're in extra time
And the other team scores
When someone informs you
There's no Santa Claus
When you gaze at the stars
And step on a nail
When you know you'll succeed
But, somehow, you fail
When your horoscope tells you
You'll have a good day
So you ask for a rise
And your boss says, 'No way.'

So my darling, my sweetheart, my dear . . .

When you spill your beer
When you shed a tear
When you burn the toast
When you miss the post
When you lose the plot
When I'm all you've got

When you break a rule
When you act the fool
When you've got the flu
When you're in a stew
When you're last in the queue
Don't feel blue
'Cause I'm telling you
I'll be there
    I'll be there
        I'll be there for you.

Louise Cuddon (1971–)

No Mistake

I know that you were made for me
And I was made for you
A wise old owl up in a tree
Told me this was true

I asked him only yesterday
If I should marry you
He answered – 'I can safely say
You're not a twit to woo.'

Martha Simms (1963–)

'No young lady should fall in love, till the offer has been made'

... no young lady should fall in love, till the offer has been made, accepted – the marriage ceremony performed and the first year of wedded life has passed away – a woman may then begin to love, but with great precaution – very coolly – very moderately – very rationally – if she ever love so much that a harsh word or cold look from her husband cuts her to the heart – she is a fool ...

... Did I not once tell you of an instance of a Relative of mine who cared for a young lady till he began to suspect that she cared more for him and then instantly conceived a sort of contempt for her? You know to what I allude – never as you value your ears mention the circumstance – but I have two studies – *you* are my study for the success, the credit, and the respectability of a quiet, tranquil character. Mary is my study – for the contempt, the remorse – the misconstruction which follow the development of feelings in themselves noble, warm – generous – devoted and profound – but which being too freely revealed – too frankly bestowed – are not estimated at their real value.

from a letter, 20 November 1840, *Charlotte Brontë* (1816–55)

A Word to Husbands

To keep your marriage brimming,
With love in the loving cup,
Whenever you're wrong, admit it;
Whenever you're right, shut up.

Ogden Nash (1902–71)

Valentine

My heart has made its mind up
And I'm afraid it's you.
Whatever you've got lined up,
My heart has made its mind up
And if you can't be signed up
This year, next year will do.
My heart has made its mind up
And I'm afraid it's you.

Wendy Cope (1945–)

The Ten Properties a Horse Shares with a Woman

The fyrst is, to be mery of chere, the seconde, to be paced, the thyrde is to have a brode foreheed, the fourth, to have brode buttockes, the fyfthe, to be harde of warde, the syxte, to be easy to lepe uppon, the vii to be good at a longe journeye, the viii to be well sturrynge under a man, the ix to be alwaye besye with the mouthe, the tenth, ever to be chowynge on the brydell.

from *The Boke of Husbandrie*, John Fitzherbert (*fl.* 1523)

'An April state of smiles and tears'

I have never seen my aunt in such state. She is dressed in lavender-coloured silk, and has a white bonnet on, and is amazing. Janet has dressed her, and is there to look at me. Peggotty is ready to go to church, intending to behold the ceremony from the gallery. Mr Dick, who is to give my darling to me at the altar, has had his hair curled. Traddles, whom I have taken up by appointment at the turnpike, presents a dazzling combination of cream colour and light blue; and both he and Mr Dick have a general effect about them of being all gloves.

No doubt I see this, because I know it is so; but I am astray, and seem to see nothing. Nor do I believe anything whatever. Still, as we drive along in an open carriage, this fairy marriage is real enough to fill me with a sort of wondering pity for the unfortunate people who have no part in it, but are sweeping out the shops, and going to their daily occupations . . .

The church is calm enough, I am sure; but it might be a steam-power loom in full action, for any sedative effect it has on me. I am too far gone for that.

The rest is all a more or less incoherent dream.

A dream of their coming in with Dora; of the pew-opener arranging us, like a drill-sergeant, before the altar rails; of my wondering, even then, why pew-openers must always be the most disagreeable females procurable, and whether there is any religious dread of a disastrous infection of good-humour which renders it indispensable to set those vessels of vinegar upon the road to Heaven.

Of the clergyman and clerk appearing; of a few boatmen and some other people strolling in; of an ancient mariner behind me, strongly flavouring the church with rum; of the service beginning in a deep voice, and our all being very attentive.

Of Miss Lavinia, who acts as a semi-auxiliary bridesmaid, being the first to cry, and of her doing homage (as I take it) to the memory

94

of Pidger, in sobs; of Miss Clarissa applying a smelling-bottle; of Agnes taking care of Dora; of my aunt endeavouring to represent herself as a model of sternness, with tears rolling down her face; of little Dora trembling very much, and making her responses in faint whispers.

Of our kneeling down together, side by side; of Dora's trembling less and less, but always clasping Agnes by the hand; of the service being got through, quietly and gravely; of our all looking at each other in an April state of smiles and tears, when it is over; of my young wife being hysterical in the vestry, and crying for her poor papa, her dear papa.

Of her soon cheering up again, and our signing the register all round. Of my going into the gallery for Peggotty to bring *her* to sign it; of Peggotty's hugging me in a corner, and telling me she saw my own dear mother married; of its being over, and our going away.

Of my walking so proudly and lovingly down the aisle with my sweet wife upon my arm, through a mist of half-seen people, pulpits, monuments, pews, fonts, organs, and church-windows, in which there flutter faint airs of association with my childish church at home, so long ago.

Of their whispering, as we pass, what a youthful couple we are, and what a pretty little wife she is . . .

We drive away together, and I awake from the dream. I believe it at last. It is my dear, dear, little wife beside me, whom I love so well!

from *David Copperfield* (Chapter 23), Charles Dickens (1812–70)

'And what of Marriage, master?'

I add my breath to your breath
that our days may be long on the Earth,
that the days of our people may be long,
that we shall be as one person,
that we may finish our road together.

Pueblo blessing

On Marriage

Then Almitra spoke again and said, 'And what of Marriage,
   master?'
And he answered saying:
You were born together, and together you shall be forevermore.
You shall be together when white wings of death scatter your
   days.
Aye, you shall be together even in the silent memory of God.
But let there be spaces in your togetherness.
And let the winds of the heavens dance between you.
Love one another but make not a bond of love:
Let it rather be a moving sea between the shores of your souls.
Fill each other's cup but drink not from one cup.
Give one another of your bread but eat not from the same loaf.
Sing and dance together and be joyous, but let each one of you
   be alone,
Even as the strings of the lute are alone although they quiver
   with the same music.
Give your hearts, but not into each other's keeping.
For only the hand of Life can contain your hearts.
And stand together yet not too near together:
For the pillars of the temple stand apart,
And the oak tree and the cypress grow not in each other's
   shadow.

from *The Prophet*, Kahlil Gibran (1883–1931)

'Silent unspeakable memories'

What greater thing is there for two human souls, than to feel they are joined for life – to strengthen each other in all labour, to rest on each other in all sorrow, to minister to each other in all pain, to be one with each other in silent unspeakable memories . . .

from *Adam Bede* (Chapter 54), George Eliot (1819–80)

Love is Giving

Love is giving, not taking,
mending, not breaking,
trusting, believing,
never deceiving,
patiently bearing
and faithfully sharing
each joy, every sorrow,
today and tomorrow.

Love is kind, understanding,
but never demanding.
Love is constant, prevailing,
its strength never failing.
A promise once spoken
for all time unbroken,
Love's time is forever.

Anon.

When Two People are at One

When two people are at one in their inmost hearts
They shatter even the strength of iron or of bronze
And when two people understand each other in their inmost
    hearts
Their words are sweet and strong like the fragrance of orchids.

The I Ching (*c.* 1000 BC)

The Art of Marriage

Happiness in marriage is not something that just happens. A good marriage must be created. In the Art of Marriage: the little things are the big ones. It is never being too old to hold hands. It is remembering to say 'I love you' at least once a day. It is never going to sleep angry. It is at no time taking the other for granted. It is having a mutual sense of values and common objectives. It is standing together facing the world. It is forming a circle of love that gathers in the whole family. It is doing things for each other, not in the attitude of duty or sacrifice, but in the spirit of joy. It is speaking words of appreciation and demonstrating gratitude in thoughtful ways. It is cultivating flexibility, patience, understanding and a sense of humour. It is having the capacity to forgive and forget. It is giving each other an atmosphere in which each can grow. It is finding room for the things of the spirit. It is a common search for the good and the beautiful. It is establishing a relationship in which the independence is equal, dependence is mutual and the obligation is reciprocal. It is not only marrying the right partner, it is being the right partner.

Anon.

For a Wedding

Cousin, I think the shape of a marriage
is like the shelves my parents have carried
through Scotland to London, three houses;

is not distinguished, fine, French-polished,
but plywood and tatty, made
in the first place for children to batter,

still carrying markings in green felt-tip,
but always, where there are books
and a landing, managing to fit;

that marriage has lumps like
their button-backed sofa, constantly,
shortly, about to be stuffed;

and that love grows fat
as their squinting cat, swelling
round as a loaf from her basket.

I wish you years that shape, that form,
and a pond in a Sunday, urban garden;
where you'll see your joined reflection tremble,

stand and watch the waterboatmen
skate with ease across the surface tension.

Kate Clanchy (1965–)

On Your Wedding Day

Today is a day you will always remember
the greatest in anyone's life.
You'll start off the day just two people in love
and end it as Husband and Wife.

It's a brand-new beginning, the start of a journey,
with moments to cherish and treasure
and although there'll be times when you both disagree
these will surely be outweighed by pleasure.

You'll have heard many words of advice in the past
when the secrets of marriage were spoken,
but you know that the answers lie hidden inside
where the bond of true love lives unbroken.

So live happy forever as lovers and friends
it's the dawn of a new life for you,
as you stand there together with love in your eyes
from the moment you whisper, 'I Do.'

And, with luck, all your hopes and your dreams can be real
may success find its way to your hearts,
tomorrow can bring you the greatest of joys
but today is the day it all starts.

Anon.

'Now you will feel no rain'

Now you will feel no rain,
for each of you will be a shelter to the other.

Now you will feel no cold,
for each of you will be warmth to the other.

Now there is no loneliness for you;
now there is no more loneliness.

Now you are two bodies,
but there is only one life before you.

Go now to your dwelling place,
to enter into your days together.

And may your days be good
and long on the earth.

traditional Apache prayer

'The love of God, unutterable and perfect'

The love of God, unutterable and perfect,
    flows into a pure soul the way that light
    rushes into a transparent object.
The more love that it finds, the more it gives
    itself; so that, as we grow clear and open,
    the more complete the joy of loving is.
And the more souls who resonate together,
    the greater the intensity of their love,
    for, mirror-like, each soul reflects the others.

from *The Divine Comedy*, Dante (1265–1321),
translated from the Italian by Stephen Mitchell

'Dear friends, let us love one another'

Dear friends, let us love one another,
because love comes from God. Whoever
loves is a child of God and knows God.
Whoever does not love does not know
God, for God is love. And God showed
his love for us by sending his only Son
into the world, so that we might have
life through him. This is what love is:
it is not that we have loved God, but that
he loved us and sent his Son to be the
means by which our sins are forgiven.
Dear friends, if this is how God loved
us, then we should love one another. No
one has ever seen God, but if we love
one another, God lives in union with us,
and his love is made perfect in us.

           from the First Letter of John
             (Good News Bible)

'Though I speak with the tongues of men and of angels'

Though I speak with the tongues of men and of angels, and have not love, I am become as sounding brass, or a tinkling cymbal. And though I have the gift of prophecy, and understand all mysteries, and all knowledge; and though I have all faith, so that I could remove mountains, and I have not love, I am nothing.

And though I bestow all my goods to feed the poor, and though I give my body to be burned, and have not love, it profiteth me nothing. Love suffereth, and is kind; love envieth not; love vaunteth not itself, is not puffed up, doth not behave itself unseemly, seeketh not her own, is not easily provoked, thinketh no evil, rejoiceth not in iniquity, but rejoiceth in truth; beareth all things, believeth all things, hopeth all things, endureth all things.

Love never faileth, but whether there be prophecies, they shall fail; whether there be tongues, they shall cease; whether there be knowledge, it shall vanish away. For we know in part, and we prophesy in part. But when that which is perfect is come, then that which is in part shall be done away.

When I was a child, I spake as a child, I understood as a child, I thought as a child: but when I became a man, I put away childish things. For now we see through a glass darkly; but then face to face. Now I know in part; but then shall I know even as also I am known. And now abideth faith, hope, love, these three; but the greatest of these is love.

I Corinthians 13 (New King James version, 1982)

Unlimited Friendliness

This is what should be done by the man and woman who are wise, who seek the good, and who know the meaning of the place of peace.

Let them be fervent, upright, and sincere, without conceit of self, easily contented and joyous, free of cares; let them not be submerged by the things of the world; let them not take upon themselves the burden of worldly goods; let their senses be controlled; let them be wise but not puffed up, and let them not desire great possessions even for their families. Let them do nothing that is mean or that the wise would reprove.

May all beings be happy and at their ease. May they be joyous and live in safety.

All beings, whether weak or strong – omitting none – in high, middle, or low realms of existence, small or great, visible or invisible, near or far away, born or to be born: may all things be happy and at their ease.

Let none deceive another, or despise any being in any state. Let none by anger or ill-will wish harm to another.

Even as a mother watches over and protects her child, her only child, so with a boundless mind should one cherish all living things, radiating friendliness over the entire world, above, below, and all around without limit. So let them cultivate a boundless goodwill toward the entire world, unlimited, free from ill-will or enmity.

Standing or walking, sitting or lying down, during all their waking hours, let them establish this mindfulness of goodwill, which is the highest state.

Abandoning vain discussions, having clear vision, free from sense appetites, those who are perfect will never again know rebirth.

from the Buddhist scriptures (c. AD 100–400),
translated from the Pali by Edward Conze

Irish Toast

May you have warm words on a cold evening,
A full moon on a dark night,
And the road downhill all the way to your door.

Notes

p. 9 'No love, to love of man and wife'. Richard Eedes was chaplain to both Queen Elizabeth I and James I.

p. 11 'And man and woman are like the earth, that brings forth flowers'. *foraminiferae*: very simple form of plant life.

p. 24 'To My Dear Loving Husband'. Anne Bradstreet was born and grew up in England but sailed for the New World two years after her marriage. She had eight children. As she had settled in Massachusetts by the time she began to write, she is often regarded as America's first poet.

p. 30 'Love Not Me'. This is, in fact, a madrigal – an unaccompanied song set for at least three but seldom more than six voices. This madrigal is in four parts. John Wilbye was one of the most important of the English madrigalists.

p. 34 'A Birthday'. *vair*: fur obtained from a black and white squirrel; one of the heraldic furs.

p. 44 'You and I'. Kuan Tao-Sheng, born in China, was also a famous calligrapher and painter. She was the wife of Chao Meng-fu, one of the most famous calligraphers and painters in Chinese history.

p. 49 'Beauty that is Never Old'. James Weldon Johnson founded the *Daily American*, the first African-American daily newspaper, and was the first black man to be admitted to the Florida bar. He wrote 'Lift Every Voice and Sing' with his brother for the celebration of Abraham Lincoln's birthday in 1900.

p. 54 'Reply'. Naomi Long Madgett celebrates the experiences of black Americans in her writings and encouraged a generation of writers and students in her work as a teacher, editor and publisher. She founded the Lotus Press, which has become a leading publisher of poetry by black writers.

p. 55 'Love's Insight'. Robert Winnett was a parish clergyman in Surrey until he retired in 1975.

p. 61 'I want to be your friend'. The Yüeh-Fu Music Bureau was established during the reign of Wu Ti (140–86 BC) in China. Originally the works were amalgams of song and poetry, but later the musical accompaniment was dropped. These poems reflected the social realities of the time and often originated from the common people.

p. 76 'The Author to His Wife, of a Woman's Eloquence'. Sir John Harington was a godson of Queen Elizabeth I. He was a writer of satires and epigrams, some of which were ill judged and caused him to suffer a period of exile from court. In an account of a visit to the Queen shortly before her death, he recounts her warning to him: 'When thou dost feele creepinge tyme at thye gate, these fooleries will please thee lesse.'

pp. 78 and 79 Sir Walter Ralegh's 'The Nymph's Reply to the Shepherd' is a response to Marlowe's 'The Passionate Shepherd to His Love', and they work well read as companion pieces, the Marlowe by a man and the Ralegh by a woman. *Philomel*: a bird; the nightingale. *kirtle*: a skirt or petticoat.

p. 102 'When Two People are at One'. *The I Ching* (*The Book of Changes*) is one of the oldest books in the world, dating back to around 1000 BC, and based on an even older shamanistic oral tradition. It is an ancient Chinese system of divination.

Acknowledgements

W. H. AUDEN: 'Twelve Songs: XII' from *Collected Poems* by W. H. Auden. Reprinted by permission of Faber and Faber.

WENDELL BERRY: 'The Dance' from *Collected Poems: 1952–1982* by Wendell Berry. Copyright © 1985 by Wendell Berry. Reprinted by permission of North Point Press, a division of Farrar, Straus & Giroux, LLC.

KATE CLANCHY: 'For a Wedding' by Kate Clanchy from *Slattern* by Kate Clanchy. Reproduced by permission of Macmillan, London.

WENDY COPE: 'Valentine' from *Serious Concerns* by Wendy Cope. Reprinted by permission of Faber and Faber.

LOUISE CUDDON: 'I'll be There' by Louise Cuddon. By kind permission of the Jonathan Clowes Agency.

E. E. CUMMINGS: 'i carry your heart in me' and 'love is more thicker than forget' are reprinted from *Complete Poems 1904–1962* by e. e. cummings, edited by George J. Firmage, by permission of W. W. Norton & Co. Copyright © 1991, by the Trustees for e. e. cummings Trust and George James Firmage.

IAN DUHIG: 'From the Irish' by Ian Duhig. By kind permission of the poet.

T. S. ELIOT: 'A Dedication to My Wife' from *Complete Poems and Plays* by T. S. Eliot. Reprinted by permission of Faber and Faber.

JAMES FENTON: 'Hinterhof' by James Fenton. Reprinted by permission of PFD on behalf of James Fenton. Copyright © James Fenton, 1993.

C. DAVID HAY: 'I'll Still be Loving You' by C. David Hay. By kind permission of the poet.

ADRIAN HENRI: 'Love is' by Adrian Henri from *Collected Poems* by Adrian Henri, Allison & Busby Ltd, 1986. Copyright © Adrian Henri, 1986. Reproduced by permission of the estate of the author

c/o Rogers, Coleridge & White Ltd, 20 Powis Mews, London,
W11 1JN.

ELIZABETH JENNINGS: 'Friendship' and 'Relationships' from *Collected
New Poems* by Elizabeth Jennings (Carcanet) by permission of David
Higham Associates.

RUDYARD KIPLING: 'The Female of the Species' by Rudyard Kipling.
By kind permission of A. P. Watt Ltd on behalf of the National
Trust for Places of Historic Interest or Natural Beauty.

PHILIP LARKIN: 'Is it for now or for always' from *Collected Poems* by
Philip Larkin. Reprinted by permission of Faber and Faber.

CECIL DAY LEWIS: 'Live you by love confined' from *The Magnetic
Mountain* by C. Day Lewis, published by Sinclair Stevenson (1992).
Copyright © 1992, in this edition, and the Estate of C. Day Lewis.

ADRIAN LOMAS: 'Wedding Day' by Adrian Lomas. By kind permission
of the Jonathan Clowes Agency.

NAOMI LONG MADGETT: 'Reply' by Naomi Long Madgett (Exposition,
1996); reprinted in *Remembrances of Spring: Collected Early Poems*
(Michigan State University Press, 1993). Reprinted by permission of
the author.

EDWIN MUIR: 'The Confirmation' from *Collected Poems* by Edwin Muir.
Reprinted by permission of Faber and Faber.

OGDEN NASH: 'Always Marry an April Girl' and 'A Word to Husbands'
from *Candy is Dandy: The Best of Ogden Nash*, edited by Anthony
Burgess (André Deutsch). Reprinted by permission of Carlton
Books Ltd.

PABLO NERUDA: 'Sonnet XVII' from *100 Love Sonnets: Cien Sonetos de
Amor* by Pablo Neruda, translated by Stephen Tapscott. Copyright ©
1986. Reprinted by permission of the University of Texas Press.

PABLO NERUDA: '. . . winter will seek us, my love' from 'Epithalamium'
by Pablo Neruda, translated by Donald D. Walsh, from *The
Captain's Verse*. Copyright © 1972, by Pablo Neruda and Donald D.
Walsh. Reprinted by permission of New Directions Publishing
Corp.

ALICE OSWALD: 'Wedding' by Alice Oswald from *The Thing in the*

116

Gap-stone Stile (Oxford University Press). Copyright © Alice Oswald, 1996. Reprinted by permission of PFD on behalf of Alice Oswald.

KATHLEEN RAINE: 'Amo Ergo Sum' by Kathleen Raine, reprinted from *The Collected Poems of Kathleen Raine*. Copyright © Golgonooza Press.

MARTHA SIMMS: 'No Mistake' by Martha Simms. By kind permission of the Jonathan Clowes Agency.

WILLIAM JAY SMITH: 'Touch the Air Softly' from *Collected Poems* by William Jay Smith. Reprinted by permission of Johns Hopkins University Press.

MARY-ANN TRACEY: 'Changes' by Mary-Ann Tracey. By kind permission of the Jonathan Clowes Agency.

ROBERT WINNETT: 'Love's Insight' by Robert Winnett from *New Christian Poetry*, edited by Alwyn Marriage (HarperCollins Religious, 1990). Reprinted by permission of Bridget Deasey.

W. B. YEATS: 'He Wishes for the Cloths of Heaven' by W. B. Yeats. Reprinted by kind permission of A. P. Watt on behalf of Michael B. Yeats.

JULIA WATSON

POEMS AND READINGS FOR FUNERALS

Words of sadness and loss, comfort and consolation.

Summoning the words to express our feelings of loss for a loved one in the days following a death can feel almost impossible. And often the choice of readings available can seem daunting.

Poems and Readings for Funerals is a carefully curated collection of the very wisest words about death by some of the world's greatest poets, thinkers, playwrights and novelists.

Featuring beautifully and thoughtfully written poems, prose extracts and prayers, these readings have been chosen to move and console, sympathize and relieve – to bring everyone attending a funeral or memorial closer together.